RelationSHIP
or
RelationSHIT

RelationSHIP
or
RelationSHIT

Which One Are You In?

Simple and Practical Ways
to Improve Your Relationships

Vince Shifflett

Printed in the United States of America

ISBN Paperback: 978-1-7359757-0-2
ISBN eBook: 978-1-7359757-1-9

Cover and Interior Design: Ghislain Viau

I dedicate this book to my mother, with whom I have always had an amazing relationship. She was my biggest fan and taught me what a true relationship should entail. I also dedicate this book to Greg, my lifelong friend who has supported me, guided me, and taught me to see my relationships in their true light—especially my relationship with myself. Your presence in my life has created unmeasurable change and increased self-awareness. I love you dearly.

Table of Contents

Foreword

My name is Gregory Dean. I am a Reiki Master, an internationally certified health coach, a teacher of energy medicine on an international stage—and, more importantly, a nearly lifelong friend of Vincent Shifflett.

It is difficult for most people—and sometimes even me—to understand how a friendship could last for more than fifty years. Vincent and I grew up going to the same church and we started the first grade in the same school. In middle school, our bond became stronger, and by the time we graduated from high school, we were practically inseparable. You can call me a witness, for I have been witness to the highs and lows, the struggles, and the triumphs of Vincent's life.

Early on, we worked at the same nursing home. During this time period, we found our first acceptance of being gay.

We worked the early shift, and Vincent needed a ride to work the next day. Therefore, he spent the night at my parent's house, and we slept in my parent's camper in the back yard. We stayed up half the night talking, which led to us coming out to each other. At that moment, by sharing what we thought was our deepest, darkest secret, we found acceptance. Through our trust in each other, we found a kinship.

After graduation, our lives took us down different paths professionally and geographically, but we were never more than a phone call away. Each of us would call the other first when we were down or had reason to celebrate. We weathered many storms and breakups, and we celebrated numerous milestones and accomplishments. At some point along the way, we realized our bond was that of *Chosen Brothers*. We chose one another as family, and more than just friends.

It has not always been all laughter and celebrations, but we decided to have the difficult conversations along the way. We have made a conscious effort to choose friendship over anything that might divide us.

Vincent is a man of many God-given talents. I have watched him grow during our long friendship. I have seen him make himself vulnerable through the truthfulness of his writing, as if standing naked in front of the world to show all of his flaws. I have witnessed the true-life teachings that he has lived, which enabled him to write this book. In these pages, you will learn from Vincent's life journey, a journey that forced him to look for the higher meanings or teachings of what relationSHIPS are meant to be.

During one of our many conversations, Vincent came up with the Title of "RelationShip or RelationShit." We have all experienced both in our lives. I am proud to have witnessed the healing that these life events have brought to Vincent. I applaud him for having the courage to share this with the world in hopes of others learning and healing through his words.

Let this book guide you through determining the status of your RelationShip or RelationShit. Allow that knowledge to heal you.

I am proud to offer my support in writing this foreword. I have seen firsthand how a RelationShit can take you to the deepest pits of despair and make you question your very own existence. If you know what to look for and understand what it took for someone else to heal, then there is hope for your own self-healing.

It is important for everyone to find their tribe, and to have RelationShips that support and lift them up, offering a soft landing when they fall and a helping hand when they need to stand back up. From my heart, I bless this writing; this Author and my dear friend, Vincent, in publishing this book; and all of those who find teaching in witnessing this writing.

With all my love and the support of a more than fifty-year friendship,

Gregory Dean

Introduction

Marriage. Children. Friends. Colleagues. Parents. What do they all have in common? Each of these is built on *relationship*. We are involved in many different types of relationships in life, including the important one we have with ourselves. We also have a relationship to the past, the environment, our coworkers, and even with God or our spirituality.

Wherever we are connected to a person, a situation, or a thing, we have a *relationship* that defines this connection. RelationSHIPS can feel full, joyful, balanced, and accepting—or they can can feel empty, sad, disconnected, controlling, or invisible. I call this latter kind a relationSHIT. Strong relationships—whether they be with other people, with our community, with our beliefs, or with ourselves—contribute to a longer, healthier, and happier life. RelationSHIPS and relationSHITS both help shape the way we think about people, places, and things. They also help us to define our own identities.

In this book, I will talk about my personal journey with relationships, good and bad, and the lessons I've learned along the way. While some experiences helped me nurture strong relationships, others helped me identify toxic relationSHITS. I am quite sure we have all experienced both types, and there are lessons to be learned from both.

Throughout the upcoming chapters, I will also challenge you to think about your personal connections and ask yourself, "Are they truly healthy relationSHIPS, or do they feel more like exhausting relationSHITS?"

Being aware of our relationSHITS gives us the opportunity to change them into relationSHIPS. In other words, it teaches us how to *get out of the shit and into the ship*. It is my deepest hope that this book will create change, stimulate self-healing, and help you develop a better understanding of your own relationships. Do they feel positive, loving, uplifting, and encouraging? Or do they feel controlling, aggressive, and disconnected?

This book will enlighten you and set you on a path to developing healthy relationships in your personal and spiritual life. It all starts with awareness.

Enjoy the read!

Chapter 1

Relationship with Self

Who are you, really? Do you love yourself? Do you appreciate your strengths? Can you pinpoint your weaknesses? If you can't answer these questions, you've come to the right place to start getting to know yourself.

Maybe you're wondering why it matters. If you don't know—and love—yourself, you'll forever hold yourself back. When you begin to understand who you are, you can figure out what excites you, how to live with purpose, and how to grow into who you want to be.

To begin, let's talk about *relationship with self.* Your relationship with yourself sets the tone and foundation for all other relationships in your life. I have spent much of my life focusing on my relationship with others, while at times completely neglecting my relationship with myself. The three most important takeaways from my journey to developing a healthy relationship with myself included:

1. Forgiving Self
2. Letting Go
3. Loving Self

Forgiving self, letting go, and loving self have taken a lot of work and tears; quite frankly, I am still in the process. In this chapter, I will present ways to forgive and find love for yourself. We have all heard the saying, "If you can't love yourself, how in the world can you love anyone else?" I have found this to be true, so let's set the foundation for self-love.

Forgiving Self

Forgiveness is an integral part of our relationship with self, as we have all done things, said things, and acted out in ways that we regret. Have you ever spoken cruel words to your spouse? Do you regret that fight you had with a friend? It is easy to carry that guilt around and continue to beat ourselves up over these past behaviors. Forgiving oneself starts with letting go of anything you did in the past.

For many years I carried around a lot of regret that also resulted in shame and guilt over being unfaithful in romantic relationships. I also felt guilt and shame about my sexual orientation and failing to live up to the "Christian" standards I was raised to believe were the only right way to live.

Learning to forgive starts with forgiving yourself. I have been my own worst enemy at times. I have berated myself for not living up to others' standards. I have beaten myself up for not achieving certain things in life. I have participated in self-loathing and negative chatter. One of my greatest challenges has been forgiving myself for harboring secrets and lies in my romantic relationships. I would blame myself for relationships that went bad. This added to my relationSHIT with myself. Only after my life started crumbling under the weight of remorse and self-loathing did I realize that I must forgive and fully accept myself in order to leave the relationSHIT behind and move into a beautiful relationSHIP with myself.

Here are some things that have helped me forgive myself:

- **Counseling**: Seek the counsel of good and wise people who support you and who have the patience to allow you time to heal in your own way. Finding a therapist proved helpful for me.

- **Meditation**: Meditation helps you cultivate a mindset of valuing all human life. This attitude will make it difficult to look at those you feel have harmed you in a negative light. Meditation will help you focus on the things we all have in common so you can value all human life, because you start to recognize that we all experience the same myriad of emotions.

- **Be empathetic:** Think about the negative emotions that you attribute to the person you feel has hurt or wronged you and recognize that they might be carrying those same negative emotions around. Try to see the situation from the other person's perspective and understand what might have contributed to their behavior, instead of judging them. This has been a true test for me. Empathy is understanding, and understanding is the first step—however, even if you cannot understand, it doesn't mean you cannot forgive. It has always been hard for me to accept that there are things I can't understand. Sometimes you have to stop trying to understand and *stand in your faith that what happens is a set of developmental challenges set forth for each of us by God.* Feeling empathy for ourselves and others allows us to take a huge step toward forgiveness because it helps us see that we all deserve forgiveness.

- **Refrain from negative talk about others:** Talking negatively about the person you feel has hurt you keeps the wound open and fresh. It's also harder to love yourself fully when you continue to carry around negative emotions such as self-loathing, regret, and shame. Think of these emotions as your teacher. Think of your situations as learning experiences, and refrain from judging the other person.

- **Find meaning in your hurt, pain, and suffering:** Ask yourself, "What lesson do I need to learn in this situation?" Seeing your circumstances as a lesson, instead of just more suffering, will lead to more self-forgiveness and ultimately a healthier relationSHIP with self. If you cannot find a meaningful lesson in your pain, perhaps you are not in agreement with God's plan or the plan set forth for you by the Universe.

- **Be patient:** It takes time to forgive yourself and others. Love yourself through the process. Forgiveness is a real gift to oneself. For me, forgiveness is about seeing the inherent worth of others, regardless of how they might have treated me. Then I can let go of the anger associated with a person or situation. Negative experiences in my life lead to negative emotions that get encoded in my memory, and every time I think about a negative experience, I feel the same negative emotions. You can break free from this loop. Forgiveness frees us to live in the present instead of the past—and besides, it's healthier. One study found that letting go and forgiving helped patients experience fewer cardiovascular and immune system problems. Forgiveness is powerful.

Forgiveness is about how we respond to "God's plan" for us. It's difficult for me to wrap my head around this at times. I have evolved into believing that everything we face in life is part of a grand development plan. Our "free will" drives the choices we make on how to respond to the plan. This is a bridge between our traditional religious/values teaching and more current views. FOR GIVING is just that. We are challenged to *give* our responses to each situation back to God or higher power. Good, bad … it doesn't matter. Being too pleased with something leads to attachment. Being too angry leads to resentment. I think our evolutionary step might be to learn to be in the middle. That doesn't necessarily mean to be indifferent, but it might be that's exactly what it takes to be in the moment. You cannot be balanced if your emotions take over. Think of the expression "FOR GIVE and FOR GET." It really means, *when you GIVE your responses back to God, you GET "grace" or enlightenment.* The space you create when we give up our emotional response and forgive is filled with God's love, which helps us on our way to further development.

How do you know when you've fully let go and been successful with forgiveness?

When you are able to think about a person or situation without feeling a rise in all the negative emotions previously attached to the person or situation, you're well on your way.

Letting Go

Letting go or releasing an experience is always a choice. Letting go is vital for our personal growth, but it can be challenging. It requires courage and faith when we can't see what lies ahead.

Many of the things we choose to hold onto keep us from growing and moving forward. I like to call them "unhealthy attachments." We might be holding onto old thoughts, past experiences, past relationSHIPS, past relationSHITS, negative emotions and feelings, or even our current relationSHIPS/SHITS. It is easy to get stuck in our comfort zone and allow fear to keep us from letting go. But when we hold unhealthy attachments, we prevent ourselves from fully experiencing the present as well as the future.

I recently left my job as a registered nurse in the hospital where I had worked in critical care environments for about thirty-two years. That job was my comfort zone, but it had turned into a bit of a relationSHIT. Even though I was used to it, I felt I needed to let go, for many different reasons. It was scary to leave. That job was all I had ever known. But I set an intention for exactly what I wanted in terms of a job and then I let it go and trusted. It is not our responsibility to worry or stress about how our dream will be fulfilled. When we set a pure intention coupled with positive emotions, the Universe will take care of the how.

One day, I received a call from an old nursing colleague/friend. We talked for a moment and got caught up on our personal lives. Then she asked me, "So, where are you working now?" I replied, "I am still working in the hospital ICU." She had an incredible opportunity for me to do something I had not done before as a nurse. I stepped out of the boat and into the water. I let go of my comfort zone. It has turned out to be a great decision that has led to new growth in many areas of my life. Don't get stuck. When something is not working, let it go.

By letting go, you make space for the infinite possibilities. As long as we have a fear of letting go of the familiar, new possibilities will not show up. As long as we have a need to understand everything, the unknown will not show up.

What are you holding onto that is keeping you from moving forward, learning, and growing? Are you in a toxic relationSHIT, or just holding onto a relationship because it is comfortable? Are you holding onto negative feelings such as anger, resentment, jealousy, or bitterness? Are you choosing to hold onto negative thoughts?

Letting go of the shit is a process. Negative thoughts and self-criticism do not make us better. They only continue to make us feel stuck and unable to move forward. Decide to let go today of whatever is not serving your highest good. Move forward, knowing that what lies ahead is something beautiful. Move forward knowing that you are enough. Choose to let go of whatever is having a negative impact on you and taking up precious mind and heart space.

Remember, new beginnings are always possible. Infinite possibilities await us all if we are able to get out of our external environment and enter the quantum unified field that is oneness. Letting go of all the shit in our past is essential for development of a healthy relationSHIP with self.

Loving Self

Our challenge is to know how much God loves all of us. If the love of God is within each of us … the "sticky stuff that holds things together" or the force that fills the 99 percent of the emptiness in our atoms—then we are all godlike … or a part of God. The challenge is to realize it. You ARE LOVED! Each of us has to learn to tune into this love to unleash our maximal potential. The more we FOR GIVE, the more we make room FOR GETTING grace. That grace can take on many forms. Things like wisdom, harmony, and understanding are the tools or gifts from God that we get when we forgive, forget, and learn to love ourselves.

For much of my life, I have struggled with bouts of depression. At times, the pain was so severe that it led me to think of ways to end my own life. All of this started in my childhood. Many factors contributed to this depression, such as the fact that I was gay and hiding it out of fear of rejection. I have learned that we are all unique expressions of God. Like the snowflakes, He created us to be unique. No two of us are the same. I am now at a place where I am grateful to be my unique self. I am grateful to the creator for making me exactly as I am.

Choices come with consequences. Some choices lead to amazing outcomes, while others lead to suffering and pain. For better or worse, each choice is the unavoidable consequence of its predecessor. Learning to love yourself is a choice, too.

My depression and lack of self-love have been the consequence of my words, thoughts, and actions. I am learning the importance of giving this back to God. It's my response to the plan set forth for my soul in this lifetime. Hard stuff. No need to look at or blame anyone else. It is the choices I, and I alone, have made that have brought me to this moment. This was a difficult reality for me to admit, but it was necessary to help begin the healing process so that I could truly love me. Blaming others doesn't solve anything. People are who they are. Are we influenced by others? Yes. Do we have a choice about how we will react? Yes. Are we in control of our own happiness? Yes.

So, where does true self-love lie?

It lies within our choices. We get the beautiful freedom to decide how or if we will be influenced by others in such a way that it steals our happiness and ability to love ourselves. We create our own experiences based on our choices. Loving self is all about what we choose to think, how we choose to act/react, and what we choose to say.

At times, I have let myself be so heavily influenced by others that I have allowed them to steal my joy. I made that choice to be influenced. The consequences were sadness, depression, self-loathing, and feeling unworthy. I allowed others to define me and to define what was lovable and what was not.

The same is true for my personal behavior and actions. I have not always made choices that were within the best interest of my personal, spiritual, and mental growth. The consequence for me was getting stuck in my emotions and spiraling downward into a depression, until it was nearly impossible to love myself. I now know it wasn't the actions themselves that caused the depression and spiraling. Instead, it was my judgment of those behaviors and actions. This has led me to understand the importance of full acceptance of myself and my actions. More importantly, it has prompted me to ask, "What's the lesson here?" Replacing self-loathing, self-judgment, shame, and guilt with acceptance, love, and understanding has led me down a path of deeper self-love.

At times, I am reminded of the story of Jonah and the Whale. Jonah made the choice to not listen to God (Spirit) and he ended up in the belly of the whale. I often feel myself asking, how many times have I chosen the wrong path and ended up in the belly of the whale? Far too many times to count.

It is easy to say, "He hurt me" or "She hurt me." The truth is, I made the choice to be hurt. That choice led to painful consequences. We tend to want to blame someone else for where we are. I am guilty of that. I am learning more and more to look inward. I am becoming more aware of the need to embrace where I am in an effort to love myself deeply. I still respond emotionally, but I try to get back into the middle zone as soon as I can by FOR GIVING (giving those emotional responses back to God) to make space FOR GETTING grace in return.

I recently found myself in a relationSHIT with some of members of my family once again. I think we all can relate. When I was explaining the situation to my best friend Greg, his response was, "Okay, what role did you play in this? What could you have done differently?" It's a challenge to look at one's self in the moment, but friends often see our situation clearly.

Every day, we are faced with thousands of choices. We make our decisions and either enjoy or suffer the consequences. These choices are often based on what we think about ourselves, the words we speak about ourselves, and how we truly feel about ourselves. Look in the mirror daily and tell yourself, "I love you." Do it even if you don't feel it. Keep this daily practice going until you do start to feel it. Words and actions really do eventually become our reality. If you do not love yourself fully and immediately, make of list of things you do love about yourself and post copies all over your apartment. Carry your list in your purse or wallet. Set it as a reminder on your phone. Put your lists in places that are easy to reach, so they can remind you of your worth. Starting a project like this is always difficult, but your list can help you change the way you think about yourself and your relationship with yourself.

My lack of love for self has often bled over into my other relationships, leading to break-ups, hurt feelings, and pain. I simply did not love anyone else fully because I still did not like the person I saw in the mirror every day. I hated myself for being a sex addict. I hated the fact that I identify as gay. I hated myself for being an unfaithful partner. I projected those emotions and feelings onto others. I developed a relationSHIT with myself.

The lack of self-love can also be looked at as ego. Tune into how much God, or the universe, is waiting for you to open the door to be loved. Bow to it. Surrender the need to love yourself. We might all be connected in the space between all the atoms in the universe by God's love. We can't access the peace, joy, harmony, and wisdom if we don't give the emotional response to God. God is waiting for these gifts, as we humble ourselves to turn loose of these emotions and let the space fill up with the grace or love of God.

Here are some things that have helped me start the process to loving myself:

- **Being mindful:** Having a constant awareness of my thoughts has helped me to become more intentional about changing them. As soon as my mind starts telling me, "You are not worthy," "He doesn't love you anymore," "They are talking about you," "You will never complete this book," "You are a sex addict," or "You are a cheater," I immediately begin to positively affirm my greatness. If we just allow the subconscious mind to constantly chatter untruths about who we really are, we start to believe them.

- **Accepting my sexual orientation:** This one was a difficult journey for me. Growing up in a Pentecostal, judgmental, condemning church brought about deep feelings of unworthiness, guilt, and shame. These feelings made it impossible for me to love myself. I felt self-loathing and worthlessness. Like me, God made you who you are. There is no right template for who we are. Your template might be more complex because of what society provides for you. All that stuff must be given back to God. You are no different than anybody else. Sexual orientation doesn't really matter, except in society's values … not God's values.

- **Be grateful:** Gratitude requires humility. Humility is accepting that, even though we might try to drive on the expressway, we keep getting drawn off and choosing dirt roads instead. Those are the relationSHITS I refer to many times in this book. There is only really one relationship: the one with your higher power. The rest is given to you to help you learn how to imbed yourself in that relationship. We must use challenges wisely for our spiritual growth and be grateful for the lessons learned.

- **Allow**: Recognize the emotions that prevent self-love and allow them to be. Acknowledge their existence and embrace them. It is important to ask, "Where are these emotions coming from?" and "What are they here to tell me?" Allow yourself to be in the moment and try to understand what brought them on. Suppressing or ignoring these emotions didn't work for me.

- **Breathe**: Inhale deeply and then exhale the emotions, releasing them. The practice of breathing and focusing on the breath creates a deeper peace for me—when I am able to accomplish it. Practice mindfully letting go as you exhale and feeling self-love as you inhale. The simple act of focusing on your breath allows you to go inward and detach from the things and situations in the external environment that have created your negative emotions.

- **Focus on your spiritual being**: It is easy to get too much into the human mind and the five senses: what we touch, smell, taste, see, and feel. We are actually spiritual beings in a human shell, but I find myself getting that twisted every now and then. The routine practice of being mindful, accepting who I am, being

> grateful, allowing, and breathwork has helped put me back in touch with my spirit. It only works for me, however, when I am consistent with those practices. The work is never complete. It is an ongoing process that we must be willing to do repeatedly to help build a healthy relationship with ourselves.

Learning to love yourself takes work, mindfulness, and practice. It does not happen overnight, so continue to work and be kind to yourself in the process.

Growing up Gay

Growing up gay in a non-accepting, non-affirming environment was a huge factor in my relationSHIT with self. I first realized I was attracted to the same sex in elementary school. I didn't know exactly what that meant at the time, nor did I understand the magnitude of that attraction. Even earlier than that, I sensed I was different. Once I understood what that meant, my life changed. I knew immediately that I could not let it be known. Homosexuality was considered the ultimate sin in my church and community. It was something you just did not talk about. Keeping all those feelings inside was difficult for me.

Hiding who I was as I went through high school was challenging. People seemed to see what I was trying to hide anyway. Kids called me names such as "fag" and "queer" in school. Then, when I got home, there was Dad. He would often call me a "momma's boy" or a "sissy." Thank God for my Mom, who always was my supporter. I think she sensed I was different, and she felt a need to protect me. And protect me she did. Even though my gay lifestyle went against her beliefs, I was her son, and love came first for not only me, but for all of her children.

I remembered thinking, who would choose to be gay? The lifestyle that was so socially unacceptable. Gay people could lose their lives just for being who they are. I prayed for many years for God to take it away and make me "straight," because the church had taught me that being gay was abnormal. Later in life, when the church did find out, they tried to anoint me with oil and cast the "demons" out of me. This only made me feel more ashamed, depressed, and isolated. I spent many sleepless nights, even as a kid, pondering my gayness. I was so confused, because my first several sexual experiences were with married men in the church—the same church that taught me that homosexuality was an abomination and a demonic spirit.

Fast forward to twenty-five years later, when I have come to realize that I am the beautiful person God created me to be. Yes, I was different than what most considered the norm at the time, but God had made me unique. Once I realized there wasn't a "demon" inside me, as the church had told me, I began to experience freedom. I accepted and loved myself exactly as I'd been created. I was not abnormal. There was nothing wrong with me.

Today, I am blessed to have some family and many friends who love me. I can express gratitude for my life. I am able to love and to express love. I am aware of the truth that we are ALL unique expressions of God, and no one is less than another. Even today, it is difficult at times knowing that certain groups of people believe that others do not deserve the same rights, just because they don't identify the same way.

It wasn't until I accepted and embraced my true authenticity that I was able to begin the process of self-love. I then was able to start building a RelationSHIP with myself, instead of a RelationSHIT. My RelationSHIP with myself has led to self-improvement, growth, and true evolution. Again, it is a continual process.

Chapter 2

My Relationship with My Sexual Being

Sex. It is how we all arrived on this planet as physical beings, right? Yet sex seems to be something people rarely dialogue about. It is almost as if it is one big secret, the pink elephant in the room that no one wants to talk about. But why? In this chapter, I will talk about my sexual addiction, because I have allowed the shame and guilt associated with that addiction to deeply affect my relationship with self. My addiction was both a search for something meaningful and a way to temporarily feel good about myself.

Sex is a powerful act. It can create beautiful life, but it also has destroyed lives. It has created immense pleasure and also unbearable pain. It has been used as an expression of love and also as an act of control and abuse.

I struggled with sex for a long time; sometimes, I still do. What should I do with my strong desires for sex and my shame and guilt after giving in to those desires? I often ask myself, what is this all about? I know I have been overly attached to sex and have used it to fill voids in my life. I have used it to find love. I am learning the importance of redirecting that yearning when I feel it. In sex, you give your body. Your body is FOR GIVING to another human being. The question is, what is going on in your mind, heart, and soul during sex? The physical pleasure is awesome, but you've surrendered to another human. I was relying on others to provide what the creator had already provided, but I didn't know another way to find it. Tuning inward was the key.

My negative emotions attached to sex began during my childhood, when sex was definitely taboo. I never even heard the word! How dare one talk about it—yet it was going on all around me. The fact that sex was taboo only piqued my curiosity and led me to want to explore it more. That exploration later created an addiction. I was taught that my sexual orientation was wrong, sinful, and terribly unholy. Of course, that led to the pain and shame I associated with sex. Later in the book, I will talk about my "disease to please" and need for validation, which also were strong contributing factors to my sexual addiction.

But first, let's talk about how it all began. At age eight, I had my first sexual experience. It was with the pastor's son behind my childhood church during a church service. It all just escalated from there. At age twelve, I was molested by a visiting evangelist who came to our church to hold a revival. During the next years, two of my mother's brothers repeatedly took advantage of me. All of my childhood molesters had one thing in common: all were men who were strongly opposed to homosexuality. Interesting, huh? This only added to my relationSHIT with the church and my relationSHIT with self.

My church had extremely restrictive rules about whom you could have sex with and when. For example, no sex was allowed on Sundays. Sex was limited to heterosexual, missionary-style couplings—with the lights off, of course. I don't know how many people followed these rules. But the bottom line is, you can't stop people from having sex, no matter how many crazy rules you have about it.

I continued to struggle with sex throughout my adult life. I have made decisions about sex that have caused me great pain and suffering. I have fought to control my sexual addiction. I've shared my body with complete strangers, as well as giving myself to someone I cared for deeply —only to discover it was just sex for him. These experiences furthered my self-loathing, regret, shame, and guilt. They left me feeling like I did not deserve to be loved.

I've realized sex is a powerful force, and when used properly, it can be a great catalyst for spiritual growth and healing on many levels. I also learned that, when I embraced sex as a spiritual act and a gift from the Universe, it brought me closer together in body and mind with another. But this requires fully embracing and accepting your sexual being, regardless of your sexual orientation. This is the part I am still working on. It is about realizing that my sexual energy is more than a rise in my anatomy and genital excitement.

I am still a work in progress regarding my ability to control my urges and spontaneous sexual behavior as I learn to love, accept, and value myself. I'm learning to see myself as worthy of true love from another. The more I fall in love with myself and cultivate a healthy relationship with myself, the less I feel the need to seek out sex to fulfill me.

Perhaps there should be more liberty and dialogue in our homes about sex. Communication might decrease some of the negative implications, like disease, shame, and addiction. Stop hiding it. Talk about it. It is part of who we are.

What Happens When the Sex Dies? Because it Will

I want to share some of my thoughts and experiences with you regarding the sexual part of my long-term relationships.

I have often asked myself, "What is the normal progression of a relationship?"

A friend and I had a conversation once about relationship progression. He said to me, "You can put a mark on the head board of your bed every time you have sex in the first year, and you won't have it that many times for the rest of your marriage."

Sometimes, he was right. My progression started with plenty of great sex, only to end up with my partner and I being friends or even strangers. What will you do when you progress to that stage? Because you will. If you've been in a long-term relationship for, let's say, five years or more, what is your sex life like? Lively? Rare? Non-existent? Are you missing that part? Looking back, the mistake I made was not talking about it when my relationships progressed to this stage. I just pretended everything was okay. It wasn't. This led to the cheating, secrets, and lies. It led to a relationSHIT.

Sex is a real part of who we are as human beings. It is an important part of life and a special way of connecting with the one you love. But what happens when the sexual connection becomes extremely rare or even non-existent?

It is easier to cheat than to have open, honest conversations with our sexual partners. Should we just suppress our sexual needs for the rest of our lives? Should you stifle the sexual part of you? This has been extremely difficult for me, as a sexual addict, to navigate.

Growing up in a Christian home, I was taught that I would meet "the one" who I would spend the rest of my life with. Then I would never think about sleeping with anyone else. During this same time, I watched my Dad cheat with every woman he could while married to my precious, devoted mother. This continued for their whole marriage until he passed away. I also saw many men in the church being unfaithful and deceitful. But how dare anyone talk about it!

When I got into relationships, I realized that there were other important components, outside of sex, and I had the innate desire to connect on that level. I learned that affection could be as intimate as sex. Lose that, and oh well. Not much hope for the relationships at that point, in my eyes. But can affection replace an intimate sexual connection? Lack of sexual intimacy might be a part of relationship evolution if both partners are amenable. Some older folks have terrific, romantic relationships without sex. They talk with each other about it. I also think some couples have health issues that might stand in the way of an actual sexual connection. That does not mean the relationship has to end. This is a new awareness for me, and I am grateful for it.

My challenge in my previous relationships was always how to fulfill my own sexual desires when sex was no longer part of my relationship. If you are unable to talk about this with your partner, then you might need to identify what is scaring you. How can you be more open to having the conversation? It is easy to say, "Oh, we've been together for twenty-five years." It is easy to pretend all is well and you are happy. But are you? Are you fulfilled? Are you getting the intimacy you desire? Longevity in a relationship means absolutely nothing if you're miserable or if you desire to be held, kissed, and made love to—and that's not happening.

I am certainly not advocating that you end your relationship. I am suggesting that you have an honest conversation with your partner and come up with a solution that works for both of you. Talking about it is a much better option than lying, cheating, hiding, having outside affairs, and being deceitful.

Sex, sexual wants and desires, and sexual behaviors are not easy conversational topics, but communication is necessary. For far too long, sex has been something no one wants to talk about. When sex dies, there's no conversation about it. People just either end the relationship, become unfaithful, or live in a sexless relationship.

I am finally at a place in my life where I am able to talk about this openly and honestly with the one I'm involved with. For the first time in a relationship, I trust. I trust and know that I can talk with him about anything. For the first time, there is no fear. It feels so much better than all the years I spent cheating, hiding, and harboring secrets. Those years ended relationships and left both parties hurt, with negative emotions.

Some things I have learned from being in relationships:

- Be honest; be honest with yourself and your partner.
- Stop pretending you're monogamous when you're sleeping with others

- Have a conversation and come up with a solution without any judgment of one another. Talking about it might lead to a much happier, more fulfilled relationship. There is no right or wrong.

- Define your relationship on your terms. Do you want a monogamous relationship, an open relationship, or a polyamorous relationship? None of these is right or wrong if they work for you and your needs. What's right is to be honest and respectful enough to have the conversations needed for a healthy relationSHIP, so you both don't fall into a relationSHIT.

After enduring much hurt, pain, shame, regret, and other negative emotions, once I fully accepted who I was, the right person showed up for me. I found someone who allowed me to be myself in all ways, including sexually, without judging and shaming me.

Chapter 3

Relationship with God

For the purposes of simplicity, I will refer to God as being synonymous with Spirit, Universe, Source, Creator, and all the other ways you might wish to refer to your higher power.

Who is God? What is God? Where is God? How do you define God? Is God a physical being or a spirit? Have you ever pondered these questions? God is everywhere, including inside the space of our atoms.

My journey of getting to know about God was not an easy path, because my church, family, and society taught me that being gay was a sin. God did not like sins, and those who sinned were dammed to hell. As I grew older, I grew to learn that God is not person but principle. The creator. The infinite.

The Eternal. God is one infinite, eternal substance. Awareness of God or truth is non-conceptual. It is beyond thought and mind. God, when stripped of all connotations and man-made definitions, is simply a placeholder for something we do not know and perhaps will never know. Whatever we think of God probably falls short of the truth.

People have different ideas, thoughts, and feelings about God. It has been the topic of many discussions and, at the same time, the cause for much division. Wars have been fought over various religious beliefs and opinions about who God is. In many situations, God became one of the most divisive features of humanity.

There seems to be so much hate and division surrounding our different views on God. God is used to promote political agendas and at times to justify hating others who do not have similar beliefs, looks, practices, and/or ideals as the dominant society.

Growing up, I was taught that God was an external being who sat "up there" somewhere looking down on me and waiting to judge me. It was almost as if God were a surveillance camera. This teaching never resonated with me, even as a child.

This teaching created fear. I was threatened with "burning in hell for eternity" if I did not accept Him as my Savior. Though my gay identity was not acceptable in my church, there were also many other rules and beliefs about God and what one's relationship with him should or should not look like. For example, women were expected to dress modestly if they wanted to have a relationship with God. In my church, we were not allowed to go to the movies, go swimming in a public pool, or wear shorts—and of course, premarital sex was out of the question. We lived under a plethora of rules set by the church. One could absolutely not have a good relation-SHIP with God if they did not abide by the rules.

My experiences do not provide me the certainty to have all the answers, but here is what they have taught me. God is a power greater than myself and His name has invoked strength in me when I am weak. His name has inspired me. My strong belief in Him has brought me to tears and provided comfort when my soul ached. I have learned God has many names, such as *I am* and *I am the Light.* He also has many forms, such as the beautiful trees, the wind that blows, the amazing assortment of animals on this beautiful planet, and the very breath we breathe. He works in mysterious and unexpected ways.

Who is God?

Considering the multiple definitions of God that humans have proposed thus far, one must conclude that the answer wholly depends on the individual. For some, He is simply a nice thought. Then there are those who only call His name during crisis or in time of need. For others, He is everything they need. His name brings comfort to those who believe. Perhaps He is the ultimate placebo: maybe even a wheelchair for those who do not realize they actually can walk alone.

Bruce Lee once said, "If there is a God, he is within. You don't ask God to give you things, you depend on God for your inner theme." This quote resonates deeply with me as it serves as a reminder that grace can fill us—if we let it. You have to let go … to forgive … to give those emotional responses back to God. Then you can be filled with grace and given more tools to help keep you tuned into the love you are seeking. You must get to a point where you know you are loved, with or without others being involved in that. YOU ARE LOVED. I believe God is within, and therefore, everything we need is within. This belief has greatly helped me to improve my relationship with God, as it allowed me to develop a greater connection to my spirit, which guides me daily to the degree that I am willing to listen and follow. I have learned that I am not separate from God. We are one.

Spiritual Litmus Test

A relationship with God (Spirit) might look different for everyone, because spirituality is so individual. For some, the relationship might involve being part of an organized religion: going to church, synagogue, mosque, and so on. For others, it might be a simple walk in nature to connect to spirit. How can one tell when they are spiritually engaged?

How do we measure spirituality? How do we measure our relationship with God?

First, it is important to distinguish the difference between religion and spirituality, as the two are often confused or used interchangeably. Religion is about practicing a certain point of view, whereas spirituality is more about feeling the divine presence. It's possible for a person to be very religious but completely disconnected from their spiritual being, leading to a relationSHIT as opposed to a relationSHIP with God (spirit). I believe this situation is prevalent in today's churches. My mother used to say, "Living in a barn doesn't make you a horse any more than going to church makes you a Christian." True Spirituality has nothing to do with religion. It is about having your own personal spiritual experience that is completely independent of others' teachings and thoughts.

My spirituality is personal. I get in touch with my spirituality a number of ways that include private prayer, meditation, quiet reflection, and walking outside. For the first time in my life, I feel a deep connection to my spiritual being that has nothing to do with my religious beliefs. The challenge I face is staying in a good spiritual place and remembering I am a spiritual being having a human experience. Too often, I have lived from my human experience as opposed to staying aware and connected to my spiritual being. I have also allowed others to judge whether I am spiritual, based on their belief system or their religion. In other words, many religious groups have judged me based on what they believe—and on their religion. Now that I am connected to a spiritual belief system, I understand exactly who I am, and I better understand my relationship with God.

The spiritual litmus test for me is obtaining inner peace and fulfillment. It is the ability to step outside of the five senses of the human experience and connect to my inner guidance. Am I always successful? Of course not. But it is my full intention to live in a place of the spirit. I try to live in a state of conscious awareness. Deepak Chopra said, "Religion is belief in someone else's experience and spirituality is having your own experience, your own relationship with God." Wow. This really resonated with me. God is consciousness.

What is your spiritual litmus test? Are you living from a place of spirit? What are some of the ways you connect to your spiritual being on a deep level? Is your experience about believing in someone else's point of view, or is it about having your own personal relationship with God (spirit)? The spiritual litmus test can be measured by thinking about your own inner peace and fulfillment. Peace comes from being connected to spirit.

God is Love

A healthy relationship with God (Spirit) must be based on love. Love is a common theme in most world religions—but is it just a word? Should it be more of an action, a behavior, and a way of life as opposed to just a word? The word seems to be carelessly thrown around. It is often used synonymously with God. We have all heard the saying, "God is love."

But if God is love, and I claim to represent God, am I exhibiting love? God is already loving other people, yet some of us have trouble finding the love. We are too involved with our world and its values. Being "in the middle" or being non-judgmental is the challenge. I believe true love is the absence of judgment.

Let's examine what the Traditional Bible says about love.

"Love is patient, love is kind. It does not envy, it does not boast, it is not proud. It does not dishonor others, it is not self-seeking. It is not easily angered and it keeps no record of wrongs" (1 Corinthians 13:4-5). Am I representing this description of love? Are you representing this description of love?

"Love is completely humble and gentle; patient bearing one another in love" (Ephesians 4:2). Am I representing this description of love? Are you representing this description of love?

The Bible speaks hundreds of times about the importance of love and equates God with love. So, if God is love, how could his name ever be used to support bigotry, hate, and injustice?

I would challenge you to look deeper at self, as I am doing, and ask yourself the following question: "Am I representing love and therefore representing God?" This question can help you cultivate a healthy relationSHIP with God.

Actions speak much louder than words. Love conquers ALL. Since God is love, it is impossible to separate the two. If you represent God, then you are commanded to love—and not just with words. It is my desire to be one with God (Spirit, Universe, Source). Being one requires that I act in love. It requires that my behavior represent love. I must admit, there are times I have failed miserably when it comes to representing love (God). There are times when my actions/reactions have been the complete opposite of love.

My awareness of my own behaviors and actions helps me maintain my relationship with God. Daily, I am becoming more aware of the necessity and desire to come from a place of love. It starts with each individual. "I am the Lord thy God. Thou shalt not put strange gods before me. Love thy neighbor as thou loveth thyself." These key commandments reflect the need to access God's loves. It's not OUR love, but rather our capacity to tune into and reflect outwardly the love of God. To do this, we must stay in the middle and remain non-judgmental.

Before every action and interaction, pause and ask yourself, does this action/reaction represent love? For those who follow Jesus, ask yourself, What Would Jesus Do in this particular situation? How would love explain your actions?

Even if you do not follow a particular belief system, love (patience, kindness) can still be the answer. I personally subscribe to spirit and leave all the man-made religious organizations out of it. Spirit will always lead in the direction of love. Using God and Spirit synonymously, the bottom line is, in order to have a healthy relationSHIP with God, we must love as he loves. When we fall into hate and division, we become disconnected from God (Spirit) and then find ourselves in a relationSHIT with Spirit.

Chapter 4

My Personal Relationship with the Church

When thinking about writing this book, one of the main questions I pondered was: "What is the true purpose of the church? This question has been on my mind for quite some time, and it has given me reason to pause. You might not agree with my perspective and thoughts, nor do you have to. But the church has been such an integral part of my journey, I simply could not write this book without talking about it.

My relationship with the church has been both a relationSHIP and relationSHIT. More often than not, it has been a relationSHIT. Church music has always been a source of inspiration to me, but the message has caused me much confusion and bewilderment. The message rarely seemed to line up with the behavior I observed from the messengers.

The church is the place where I have experienced the most hurt, rejection, judgment, condemnation, and drama. This truly felt like a relationSHIT. On the other hand, I have formed long-lasting connections with beautiful people from church. I've felt connected to my spirit at times, and I've been inspired. This felt more like a relationSHIP.

The physical structure of a church, along with its many denominations, is all man-made. Man created Baptist, Methodist, Science of Mind, Pentecostal, Christian, Catholic, and the many other names (labels) we use for our different religious organizations. But, what makes one better than another? What makes one right and one wrong? Isn't the message supposed to be the same?

These various man-made denominations have divided us. They have caused wars and created hatred among the religious systems, as individuals believe that their way is the right way. What happened to the traditional Scriptural instructions to "let every man work out his own soul salvation?"

There was a time when the church was run completely by servants. The offerings were used to feed the hungry, shelter the homeless, and clothe the poor—not to pay salaries for church employees. When I was a child, the pastor of my church had a full-time job. He pastored the church with no salary. It was his calling, not his job.

Fast-forward to now, and we find a lot of energy around the whole money issue. I've noticed that thirty minutes of any given service is spent talking about money—how much is needed, and all the ways you can give your money. Then there are advertisements from the pulpit about all things for sale, such as classes, books, videos, and concerts as well as many different types of services offered.

For me, it was difficult to hear the real message because they were drowned out by the commercials, which kept interrupting the regularly scheduled program.

Then, of course, there was always a little fear thrown into those pulpit messages. They said you will not be blessed unless you give. The church uses fear as a means of control, using biblical Scripture to back it up. They tell you if you don't believe exactly as they do, "you're going to hell." Is the purpose of the church to instill fear in its members? Knowing and witnessing all of this has led me down a path of negative feelings, which in turn has created a relationSHIT between the church and me.

With the move toward mega churches, church leaders have begun driving nicer cars, flying on private planes, and living in mansions, even while many in their congregations struggle to eat and pay bills. There is certainly nothing wrong with blessing others monetarily—but has the church gone too far?

When I was a child, my family and I used to travel and minister in churches all along the northeast. The churches we would minister in would take up a "love offering" to help us with our expenses. It was always barely enough to cover the gas it took to get to the next church. I am aware that it takes money to run the church. But I wonder—Are we being good stewards of the money coming in through the offering plate?

Just think what the church could do with all the money pay out in salaries. How many more people could the church help? How much more could it fulfill its true purpose of serving those in need? Could those salaried positions be filled with people who do the work merely to be a blessing, expecting nothing in return? My intent is not to be critical of the church, but to ask myself these questions. Do churches need to be multi-million-dollar buildings with $60,000/month operating budgets, or should they be more humble abodes filled with people ready to serve? Should there be churches at all? Again, the people are the church—not the building.

I personally made the decision to give my money directly to those in need instead of having a portion of it going to pay church salaries. I am a giver by nature, and I believe "You reap what you sow." I am just learning to evaluate where my money goes. I want my giving to feed the hungry and be a blessing to those less fortunate. Giving back is essential.

Growing up in the Church

My mother had me in church every Sunday morning, Sunday night, and Wednesday night, along with frequent, weeklong revivals throughout the year. I loved being with her, but I never resonated with the message itself. As I got into my younger adult life, I became the church piano player. It was not a paid position. I did it because I felt a call to do it, and I loved it. The music was always my favorite part of the service.

I remember watching as women would "dance in the spirit" and shout the bobby pins out of their hair during the music. As kids, we would see who could collect the most bobby pins from the floor at the end of the service. I remember thinking while watching them dance and shout, "God, is that you?" The issue for me was, the people shouting the loudest were also the ones who did the most gossiping, causing drama in their families and on their jobs, cursing the cat and kicking the dog at home. Simply put, they were different people in everyday life. Inside the church, they were heaven-sent. Outside the church, they had brunch with the devil. Their behavior confused me as a child, and it does even today. Having said all of this, I do also recognize that some people truly connect to the God within by shouting their bobby pins out. Whatever works is valid, as long as worship is not the goal. The *connection* should be the goal—and people connect in different ways.

The church deacons, board members, pastor, and everyone in the church loved me to death. I was quite a popular figure in the church, eventually also leading the youth choir. But once the church found out I was gay, everything changed. That love became conditional. It became, "we love you, but..."

One day the pastor called me to his office to talk. He cried and I cried. As we began to talk, my lips began to quiver while trying to hold back the tears. He was a very loving man who was more like a father to me. Pastor Pressley informed me that the deacons told him I must be removed from the piano bench and my role at the church, because I was gay. That was one of the most hurtful days of my life. He then hugged me and said, "I told them, you aren't going anywhere." While I had the support of Pastor Pressley, I never felt the same about church after that.

I remember being anointed with oil and church leaders trying to cast the "gay demons" out of me. Their fear tactic was working. I was terrified. But that anointing left me feeling ashamed, alone, guilty, depressed, hopeless, and at times, suicidal. I tried so hard to change my sexual orientation so I could "go to heaven" and not hell, because I wanted to be accepted by the church.

A few weeks after my meeting with the pastor, two of the female worship leaders, to whom I was very close, showed up at my house. When they pulled into my driveway, I looked out the window and smiled, thinking they were just coming to see me. We all sat down in my modest, peaceful living room. Much to my dismay, they informed me they could no longer sing with me—because I was gay. I could feel my heart begin to flutter as once again, the tears filled my eyes. I felt a deep pain and hurt.

I never went back to church after that day. I maintained a beautiful relationship with my pastor, but never attended another service there.

About a month after I stopped going to church, the deacon who had been at the center of the decision to oust me was arrested in an undercover prostitution sting. I have watched, time and time again, as church leaders judged and condemned me for being gay while they were partaking in their own secret sins. This also brought an awareness to the hypocrisies in my own life. I wasn't being my true authentic self, either, largely due to fear of unacceptance and ridicule.

Several years later, when I moved to Atlanta, I found an affirming congregation that was inclusive and loving. I attended for about three years before I made the decision just to leave organized religion. Church had become a distraction for me, a distraction away from my spirit. It felt more like a business, a live concert, a fashion show, or a courtroom with lots of judgment. Church seemed to be a neighborhood with lots of gossiping or simply a gathering place for friends.

I remember attending church in Atlanta one Sunday, and the whole band was missing except for the piano player. After the service, I asked the pastor, "Where's the rest of the band?"

She replied, "We could not afford to pay them this Sunday, so they did not come." Wow! They didn't even attend the service. That stuck in my heart and saddened me. It once again put a bad taste in my mouth and further led to the relationSHIT I had developed with religion.

I also finally came to realize that I do not need the physical structure of an organization to have a spiritual experience and deepen my walk with God (Spirit). I can wake up any morning and have a beautiful spiritual experience by taking a walk in the park, giving thanks, meditating, volunteering in my community, and/or just spending time in silence.

Has the church lost sight of its true purpose? I love the church, but I believe it should be a center that takes care of the community and those in real need. It should be a center that loves and welcomes ALL.

You are the church. I am the church.

We can each do our part to fulfill the true purpose of the church by:

- **Reaching out to those in need**
- **Volunteering in the community**
- **Loving ALL and practicing inclusivity**
- **Being kind to ALL of God's creation**

Each individual can do that without belonging to an organized religion created by man. There is certainly nothing wrong with belonging to a church, if that is what one chooses to do. Personally, I just found that a deep evaluation of my purpose was necessary.

My sanctuary is inside of me.

The Church: Is it a Dying Organization?

My mother raised me in church, and for that, I am grateful. We went to church so often, it felt like my second home. Things have certainly changed. Could it be that the physical building we call the church is a dying organization?

Looking back on the church, I have realized some disturbing truths about this organization that have led me to ponder many questions.

- **Who is God?**
- **Where is God?**
- **Is God separate from us?**
- **Aren't we all just ONE universal Spirit?**
- **Where is this Hell I've been told about?**
- **Where is Heaven?**

Do I have all the answers? Not by a long stretch. I ask these questions to also provoke thought in you. And remember, the mind, heart, and spirit are much like parachutes: They only work when they are open. It is my hope you will keep your mind, heart, and spirit open as you think about what your answer would be to these questions.

Perhaps God is not who you've been taught your whole life He is. Perhaps God is not where you have been told He is. Are Heaven and Hell really physical destinations?

For centuries, the church has used fear tactics to get people to follow—but follow who? They have preached that if you don't "get saved" and follow Jesus, then you will go to hell and burn forever. So, where is this "Lake of Fire" where thousands of "sinners" are burning forever, yet never burn up? Where is it located?

Where is this place called Heaven that "Christians" go after they die? Do people really go somewhere and walk on streets of gold forever? Sounds like a nice story, but is it reality?

Could it be that Heaven and Hell are not physical destinations at all, but rather states of mind, with each day bringing a new opportunity to choose which one we will be in? My choices have led to many days in hell, but I've also had many euphoric days in heaven.

Church has been both a place of inspiration and a place of great hurt for me. The gossiping, deceitfulness, extreme hypocrisy, fear tactics, and fairytales were discouraging. I could write a book just on my experience in the church. Is the church too much of a business, bank, social gathering, fashion show, Broadway musical, or perhaps a place to hide who you really are?

Many politicians have used the church as a platform to win elections. They have even come to the church to solicit votes and sell promises of a better life. "Oh, he's a Christian, so I'm voting for him." I think we have all seen behavior that is far from Christian coming from the highest office in the land—yet the Christians continue to support this behavior by casting their vote.

Next time you attend your church, look around. What is the majority age group represented in the church? More than likely, it is not millennials. Is it possible that they have chosen to also ask themselves these important questions? The millennials do not seem to be buying into the fear tactics, the drama, and the stories being told.

Each of us has the power to discover our own spirit and our own path without all the drama of the church. It is my belief that people are more awakened to the fact that the sanctuary is inside of them and not inside a building where they are preached at, condemned, and judged.

I certainly respect those who believe in the traditions they were raised to believe. I respect those who choose to attend church. But I have to wonder, is the church serving its true purpose? Quite frankly, I see more spirituality in people who do not attend church. The Bible has been terribly distorted by many men to make it mean what they want it to mean and to justify their bigotry and hate.

What would happen if the church practiced more love and less fear? What would happen if the church practiced more acceptance and less judgment? What would happen if there was more authenticity and less hypocrisy? What would happen if they fed the hungry instead of buying the pastor a new Mercedes?

I have served at the top of large church organizations. Oh, the things I saw, heard, and experienced! It was one thing in the pulpit and another out. I saw families arguing and not loving each other. I've seen churches split, as certain groups fighting with other groups in the church held elections to vote people in and out of positions. These groups used parts of the bible to judge and condemn others. This was more of the relationSHIT part of the church for me.

Chapter 5

My Relationship with the Man Known as my Father

I never once heard the words, "I love you," "I'm proud of you," or any other affirming positive messages from the man known as my father. It felt like we were strangers living in the same house. I never felt his touch. Now I realize that perhaps he did not know how to reflect God's love toward me, and there were reasons for that.

I grew up with three siblings who seemed to all be the "apple of his eye." He would take my brothers hunting and fishing and spend time with them. He would laugh with them and talk with them. It was the same with my sister. He adored her and always made sure she knew it through both his gestures and words.

I know I wasn't a perfect child, but he would find a reason to beat me aggressively using whatever he could find to beat me with. I saw the pain in my mother's eyes each time, but she felt her hands were tied. She was a strong Christian woman who truly believed the man was the head of the house. She didn't think she had any authority to step in and protect me.

My father often called me a "sissy." He would tell me to "go suck my momma's titty" or put on her dress. He seemed to hate the strong bond I shared with my mother. He also hated that I was gay, although I had not come out at that point. He sensed it. I am trying to understand that perhaps he didn't hate me. Maybe, just maybe, he didn't know how to handle my sexual orientation and it was simply his worldview regarding homosexuality that led him to abuse me.

He was also an unfaithful husband to my mother, which only added to my relationSHIT with him. I was angry with him for cheating on her and disgracing her. He slept with and/or touched every female he could get his hands on. Apparently, that was okay—but being gay was not. My mother unfortunately repeated the pattern with her second husband, but that's a completely different story that we won't talk about in this book. Looking back on my "father's" unfaithfulness to my beautiful mother, I now know he also had a void in his life he was trying to fill.

As I got older, I noticed that I started mimicking some of his behaviors. I realized that I was starting to become exactly like the man known as my father, as I too have cheated and been unfaithful in relationships. I realized that we were both trying to fill a void. This realization allowed me to better understand and let go of the anger I held toward him. I wept at this realization. How could I be angry with him or hate him when I was, in fact, so much like him?

The man known as my father died at age forty-two of a massive heart attack. I felt a sense of relief, both for myself and my mother. Perhaps we both could finally live a life of peace and be our true authentic selves. Perhaps now we could enjoy life more. My siblings were distraught over his death, which made sense, given their relationships with him. Along with feeling relieved, I also felt a different type of pain. I hurt for the relationship I'd never had with him.

After his death, I began to see my mother blossom. She started taking better care of herself. She began wearing make-up and earrings, fixing herself up, and taking pride in herself. She just appeared happier—until she met and married another man who was just like the man known as my father.

After my father's death, a weight was lifted off my shoulders. I began to feel free to live my life more authentically. I began living in my truth as a gay man, without fear of his continued rejection, judgment, and retaliation.

I have finally been able to release all the emotions tied to the relationSHIT I had with the man known as my father. Taking a closer look at myself and the commonalities we all share was an epiphany moment for me. We all walk our own journey. We all stumble and fall.

It is only when we are able to forgive, let go, and love that we find true inner peace and abundance. That continues to be my motivation and intention.

Who was my father?

I was told by my grandparents on both sides, and other family members, that the "man known as my father" was not my biological father. Several other family members confirmed the story. I will share the story with you.

My mother and the man known as my father separated for approximately one year before I was born. During that year, he fathered another child by another woman, and my mother became pregnant with me by another man. I never discussed my birth with either my mother or the man known as my father, mainly because I did not want to hurt her or make her feel embarrassed for what happened. I know that was the reason she never talked with me about it.

The resentment and hate I felt from the man known as my father was undeniable. Once I heard the story of my birth, it validated my feelings and his treatment of me. Perhaps he hated me because I was not his biological child. But given my close bond with my mother and my gay identity, I guess it was just too much for him to love me. Regardless, I think it was primarily his worldview that drove his behavior toward me. If I had fit his definition of a perfect son, we might have been able to get along fine. That was part of what both of us got on our soul growth plan … a brutal path.

At his funeral, I met his son by the other woman. I didn't quite know what to say. I did not really know him. However, that too was validation that the story I had heard was true.

How did my relationship with my father affect my relationships moving forward?

The relationSHIT with the man known as my father left me feeling unworthy of love. My relationSHIT with him mentally wired me to believe I did not deserve love. My future relationships were impacted by the thought of unworthiness he ingrained in my brain. When another man tried to show me love, I ran. I really did not know how to accept love. I still feel undeserving and unworthy at times.

Healing from that Relationship

It has taken me much of my life to come to terms with the lesson from the relationSHIT with the man known as my father. It has taken work, therapy, meditation, energy work, prayer, and counseling. Quite frankly, there are days when my memory still takes me back, and the emotions are right there, too. I am learning to live in the present. I have also learned that emotions are tied to experiences, and as long as we re-live those experiences, we will continue to have those same emotions. We are essentially living in the past instead of living in and enjoying the present. *Gratitude and forgiveness* are important to the healing process. Having said that, I am grateful to the man known as my father for being a hard-working man. I remember he hand-built all the cabinets in our kitchen. He was quite the handy man around the house. My relationSHIT with him brought an awareness to me of the similarities we all share, and it created more compassion in me. I thank him for that lesson.

My daily practice of meditation, coupled with my conscious state of awareness, helps me to remain present—but I am still a work in progress. When I think about the past experiences with the man known as my father, I immediately bring my awareness back to myself, my breath, and my present moment. It is constant work, but I am deeply grateful to be in the now. I'm grateful for the knowledge and truth that I can continue to heal myself from the past. I am also grateful that the man known as my father taught me to survive all of his bullshit, which helped prepare me to survive in this world and in my life. Life can be challenging, just as my relationship with him was challenging. I learned survival skills as a result. To him, I give thanks for that. My gratitude and forgiveness are helping me move beyond that experience and into my higher self. I'm grateful for all the lessons he taught me. He taught me that we all have our struggles, and we are similar in so many ways.

Chapter 6

My Relationship with my Mother

My mother was my everything. Her love for me was palpable. Just being in her presence put my heart and mind at ease. Despite the many challenges she faced in her life, she remained an amazing mother to me and my siblings.

The special bond I shared with her was made deeper by our shared love for music. I think she felt a need to protect me a little more. She would always say, "I am so proud of you and everything that you are." Even while others judged me, she stood by me with the strongest of love and support.

I remember looking out into the audience during my graduation from nursing school and seeing a tear trickle down

Mom's cheek. She was so proud. I was equally as proud of her. Everything I did, I did to make her proud. My accomplishments were inspired by knowing how proud she would be. It was my intention to always make her proud.

I have great memories of us playing music together, cooking together, laughing together, shopping together, and the daily phone conversations we had. Sometimes my phone would ring five minutes after hanging up with Mom. Mom would say, "What are you doing?" I would reply, "The same thing I was doing when we spoke five minutes ago." We would both laugh. I loved our phone conversations. She would call me on her way to work each day and I would call her on my way home. She would talk me through recipes on the phone until the dish was complete. Of course, mine never turned out like hers. She was an amazing cook.

There was almost NOTHING I did not share with her. She might not have always agreed with my actions, but she still loved and supported me. She encouraged me during the challenging times in my life, especially when other family members would judge me for being gay. Mom stood by me.

Coming out happened one night shortly after we moved from Elkton, Virginia to Asheville, North Carolina. I was in heaven. Small town boy moved to a bigger city. Shortly after the move, I discovered a gay club. I was both nervous and excited, as I had never been inside a gay establishment before.

I decided to go one night. When I pulled into the parking lot, I could hear the music playing inside the club. I will never forget it. The disc jockey was playing, "It's Raining Men." I immediately felt a joy and acceptance I had not felt previously in my life. I no longer felt like an outcast. I was grinning from ear to ear. I felt like I was home, with my people. I could go in and fully be my true, authentic self. What a great feeling of freedom.

That night, I lost my car keys in the club and ended up having to call Mom at two a.m. "Where are you?" she asked.

"I am at the Cock-a-too."

"Where?"

I explained to her how to get there and she said, "I am on my way." It took her about fifteen minutes to arrive. When I got in the car, I apologized to her. She was calm and loving as always. We had a conversation on the way home, and I told her it was a gay club. Her only advice was, "Be careful." There were no other questions, and our relationship continued on as normal. She let me know through her actions that it was okay to be who I was.

The Phone Call that Changed me Forever

It was a chilly day in April 2012. Mom and I talked on my way to work, as we had always done. It was a busy day at work, but around eleven a.m., I felt the urge to call her from my cell phone. There was no answer. I immediately felt a heaviness in my heart, but I continued working. About an hour later, my cell phone rang, and I recognized it as a number from Asheville, North Carolina, the city where Mom still resided. While I recognized the area code, I did not know who was calling. My heart dropped, as this was unusual.

It was my niece. She said, "Grandma has been in a bad car accident and is in surgery now to stop the bleeding." Being a nurse, I knew this was not good. I was inconsolable. The woman who was my everything now was in surgery with her life on the line. I couldn't imagine life without her.

I jumped in my car and called my room-mate/ex-partner. He was also very close to my mother, as he and I had shared eighteen years together. He met me at the house and offered to drive me to Asheville. I said, "I will try to make it." I was crying, screaming, shaking, and completely distraught. I threw some clothes in a bag and hopped in my car.

As I drove, I phoned my brother Forrest. He answered and there was a long pause. He said, "Momma didn't make it." I slammed on my brakes, almost crashing my car. I pulled over, screaming, and called my roommate back. I drove back home, and he ended up driving me to Asheville. The pain in my heart was like no pain I had ever felt before. I was in disbelief. I am grateful that I had his love and support during the most difficult time in my life. Thank you, Cedric.

I spent the next three months out of work and in therapy. I was suicidal. I believed that I could not live without her. My therapist and my best friend Greg were instrumental in getting me to a place where I no longer wanted to die. I feared for my own life, crying day and night for months. I was truly on rock bottom.

Eight years later, I am finally starting to realize that I had forty-nine years with the MOM of all MOMS. Recognizing and honoring that has helped me to change my perspective. Instead of the grief from losing her, I know I was blessed to have her. She was not just my Mom; she was my best friend.

My mother's departure from this world in her physical form was the most painful experience of my life. I lost all fear of death when she passed. So much so, that I even lost the fear of taking my own life. It was a scary time for me. I wanted to die, but at the same time, I was scared I was going to commit suicide. Over time, and with therapy, I have learned that I can still talk to her whenever I need her presence. No one ever completely gets over that kind of loss, but it's possible to learn every day to live with it.

Rock Bottom

We have all heard the expression, "rock bottom." It implies that there is nothing but rocks on the bottom. No green grass. No beautiful flowers. No amazing landscape. Just hard rocks. Have you ever felt like you're down there, on the bottom? Did you ever feel as if you're all tangled up in your emotions and can't see your way clear? These have become all too familiar feelings and thoughts for me. By definition, the bottom is the lowest or deepest part of anything. That is exactly where I was after my Mother's tragic death. I was back in a relationSHIT with myself.

Is it necessary to hit rock bottom? Is it necessary to feel like you're at the end? There are certain lessons to be learned on the bottom, but it's also important to realize that the rocks on the bottom can be beautiful. They can be just as beautiful as the green grass, colorful flowers, and amazing landscape.

Way too frequently in my life, I have felt raw with pain on the inside. Yes, I often write about and promote positivity. However, I must admit that at times, it is a struggle for me to stay off the bottom. My ability to move upward toward the surface and away from the bottom is met with fear and meaningless mental chatter. It was no different after my Mom's death. The mental chatter and fear kept me on rock bottom for a long time.

I allowed my thoughts to get caught up in a repetitive loop of negative thinking and emotions. I often wondered how to untangle myself from the emotional mess and muster up the energy to swim to the surface. I concluded that my unresolved feelings, thoughts, and continuous unhealthy choices (behaviors) were keeping me on the bottom. Yet even with this knowledge, I still find myself on the bottom. Laying on the rocks. It's not exactly comfortable. I know that I must give my unresolved feelings and unhealthy choices back to God. Again, when we give it all back to God, we create space for newness and love.

My unhealthy choices included going back to that relationSHIT. Continuing to hang out around negative energy, in an unhealthy work environment. Continuing to eat unhealthy food and not exercising. All these choices affected my mental state and led me back to the bottom. These choices—coupled with unresolved feelings such as fear, worry, and hurt—kept bringing me back to the bottom. They still keep me tangled up in this emotional mess when I allow them to. The fact that those unresolved feelings, emotions, and unhealthy choices were the reason I ended up on the bottom was not enough. I realized I would need to take consistent action. As I have matured and grown, I have learned a few ways to deal with my unresolved feelings and emotions. The habits listed below have worked for me. Use them as you see fit, but find ones that are important for you.

- **Energy Work**
- **Meditation**
- **Counseling**
- **Forgiveness**
- **Gratitude**
- **Compassion**

I knew I should not view my Mother's death as final. I knew I needed to realize and feel that her spirit was still alive and very much with me. I knew I must be more aware of my every thought and work to change it. Sounds like an easy fix, huh? But it takes work, awareness, consistent action, and commitment.

Remember that the bottom is an opportunity to look up at the top. The end is really just the beginning. When the second hand on the clock makes it to twelve, it signals the end of one minute and the start of another. When you are on the bottom, keep in mind that you have the power to change it all. Be encouraged that whatever you are going through has a time limit and will pass. Keep pushing and reach for the sky. Reach for what it is that you long for and desire. You are not intended to stay on the bottom. We all get there, but we do not have to stay there. Learn the lesson and swim like hell back to the top, where you belong.

What helped me swim back to the top was realizing that my Mom's body was the only thing that was gone. Her spirit was very much alive, and she was with me daily. Her spirit continues to guide me and be a light for my path. We don't always understand, but when we simply trust, it brings peace. The process took me a long time.

If you are on *Rock Bottom,* start stacking the rocks and build a staircase back to the top.

Chapter 7

Relationship with Friends

The old saying, "In order to make friends, you must FIRST show yourself friendly" goes back to my belief that what you put out, you get back. The energy you send out comes back to you. Regardless of whether a friendship is intimate, platonic, soul-mate, acquaintance, or otherwise, there will be a beginning, middle, and end. Most people come into your life for a season, with a few exceptions. There are always a few life-time friends. That special life-time friend for me is Greg.

Greg and I met during the first grade in elementary school and have been inseparable since. To date, we have fifty-two years of much more than a friendship. He is the one human on this earth who knows more about me than anyone else.

To this day, he remains my counselor, health coach, mentor, editor, brother, and best friend. There is no doubt in my mind that I might not still be in this physical world had it not been for his interventions and love. He has always been a good listener, loyal and non-judgmental. All these qualities are important in friendships.

We all need friends like Greg.

It is also important to have a network of friends. That network might change as you grow. One Harvard study concluded that having solid friendships promotes good brain health, reduces stress, and allows us to rebound from health issues and diseases more quickly. A friend network contributes to a positive relationSHIP with self. Friends help you celebrate the good times while being a great support during the bad times.

Most people come into your life for a purpose and with a lesson to be learned. We can learn something from every person we encounter, including the homeless man on the street, the barista at the coffee shop, and the cashier at the grocery store. Everyone is our teacher to the degree we are willing to learn. It is the same with friends. We learn and grow from each other.

I see friends as an exchange of love; a giving and receiving. Friends might not be around forever. Sometimes, they learn what they need to learn and move on to another friend, where they can continue to grow. This works both ways. You might move on as well if you discover you no longer need a FriendSHIT friend. Or you might move on as part of your growth—not away from a FriendSHIT, but toward another opportunity. We only have so much time. You can always circle back to older friends as you progress in learning.

When you discover that the Friendship has transitioned into a friendSHIT, it is time to move on.

If you are not feeling loved, uplifted, supported, and encouraged in your relationship—whether it's with your family, your church, your job, or your circle of friends—just move on. Move to a space where you can keep growing. Find a place where the energy is elevated and lifts you up.

That space could very well be your mind, as previously discussed, in terms of what energy you are sending out. But it is still important to surround yourself with loving, supportive, encouraging, and uplifting people.

If you are in a friendSHIT where you are always the one giving, and you feel drained and used—or you are feeling negative energy every time you are with that friend—it is time to move on to more productive, fulfilling friendSHIPS. They are essential.

Also, if you recognize a relationship pattern, consider why it happens. I have found some of this to be related to my ability to be honest in the relationship from the get-go.

At times, I have been more focused on sexual attraction, and I've let the friendSHIP part slide because I liked the sex. Eventually, that becomes clearer, and you notice.

In thinking about your own personal friendships, ask yourself:

- Is this friendship one-sided?
- If this is a friendSHIT, what is the shit trying to teach me?
- Is the friendship a lesson, a blessing—or maybe both?

I have been blessed with many wonderful friends and I am deeply grateful for that.

Chapter 8

Relationship with My Personal Companions

What constitutes a good romantic companionSHIP? What leads to a romantic companionSHIT? Healthy companionships involve intimacy, passion, communication, compromise, and commitment. It takes two to have any sort of relationship. There will be times when both are in the ship, and times when both are in the shit. That is just the reality. No relationship is perfect.

I have been blessed to have had several long-term intimate companionships. Some have turned out to be companion-SHITS, while others have been beautiful companionSHIPS. I have learned a few lessons along the way that I hope will benefit you.

When my eighteen-year relationship ended, eight years ago, I had several unsuccessful romantic companionships. Why was that? Eighteen years is a long time to be in a relationship. Once that connection ended, I beat myself up over it for a while. I had a negative outlook on future companionships. I blamed myself until I realized, "it takes two." But it made me consider how long had the two of us been drifting away from each other before the relationship/companionship "went south." How many years was it okay?

Remember, we are all constantly evolving. It can be challenging to stay with one person when both of you are evolving. The key, for me, is to try to talk about it. Talk about how you are changing, and get feedback on how the other person feels about the changes.

I went back and read many of the articles I wrote over the last three years. In one, I talked about saving myself for that special one, and how important I thought monogamy was once I met that special one. I went on to passively judge those who did not believe that way.

Fast forward to a year later, and I had penned an article that pretty much said monogamy is hypocrisy. What is it I truly believe? What is it I truly want? Do I want what society has taught me my whole life is the right thing—the partner, the house with the white picket fence and two dogs where you live happily ever after? Actually, I was taught I needed a *wife* to live happily ever after. That might work beautifully for some, but not for all.

The biggest lesson I am learning is that **WE ARE NOT ALL THE SAME.** And that's okay.

I used to go back and forth with what it is I wanted. Perhaps that was part of my struggle with making decisions regarding relationships. I recognized it was way past time for me to be honest with myself. It was time for me to truly love myself and to accept self without shame and judgment from myself or others.

I knew I needed to be okay with exactly where I was in the moment. My worrying, anxiety, and stress over desiring a "healthy relationship" actually was keeping it away. I also began to realize that my definition of "healthy relationship" was evolving. I realized it was essential for me to be aware of and fully understand my own definition and accept it as who I was.

When we know and accept exactly what we want, the right one will show up. Once you know what you mean by a healthy relationship, the one who aligns with your definition of a healthy relationship will show up. Even if you don't agree on everything, it's important for two people who decide to enter into a commitment to have similar definitions or what a good relationship looks like. I have listed what is important to me in terms of a Healthy RelationSHIP versus a RelationSHIT.

Healthy RelationSHIP:

- Trust
- Open communication
- Meaningful conversation
- Romance
- Affection
- Acceptance and allowing
- Respect
- Friendship
- Laughter
- Maintaining outside relationships and interests
- A healthy balance between dependence and independence

RelationSHIT:

- Judgment
- Disrespect
- Being a parent instead of a partner
- Playing detective and spying on your partner
- Deceitfulness/hiding/sneaking
- Secrets
- Lack of completely honest communication
- No romance or affection
- Lack of fun, joy, and laughter
- Unhealthy expectations of yourself or your partner
- The need to be right
- Fear-based emotions such as jealousy

TRUST is foundational to ALL RELATIONSHIPS. My lack of trust undermined my ability to communicate with my partners. Sometimes, we don't trust that the other person will choose to be in a relationship with us if we are totally honest with them. I lacked the trust that my partner would stay in a relationship with me if I was totally honest with him about my needs and about exactly who I was. I held back from expressing those needs out of fear of losing him

Dis-Ease to Please

For most of my life, I have been afflicted with the "*Dis-ease to Please,*" particularly in my romantic relationships/companionships. My need to please has too frequently made me unable to say no. But where did my disease to please come from?

Needing to please comes from a place of fear. I feared not being accepted if I didn't please. I feared being alone if I didn't please. I also felt the fear of hurting someone or even losing my job if I said no. I didn't trust them, and I didn't think I would be accepted. This is a challenge in ALL RELATIONSHIPS! LACK OF TRUST is the basis for relationSHIT, in my opinion.

My disease to please goes as far back as my childhood. It comes from a place of deep insecurity. I felt I wasn't good enough or worthy enough to please myself, so I spent most of my childhood trying to please the man known as my father. I wanted his love and acceptance so much. Unfortunately, I never got it. I wanted to please the church by trying to be who they taught me I should be, instead of being my true, authentic self. I was also constantly careful not to disappoint my mother, who saw me as her good son.

In reality, it all boils down to self-acceptance and self-worth. I did not value myself enough, and therefore I did not think I was enough. If I knew I was enough, I would not need to please to be accepted.

I am learning that it is perfectly okay to say no. Saying no and putting myself first is not selfish at all. It is essential. This requires an evaluation of my relationships. Is it okay to want to please? Absolutely. Any time I am able to make someone smile or add to their life in a positive way, that's a good thing. But when I am unable to say no and feel I must go against what my spirit is telling me, it becomes a problem.

I have suffered from the disease to please in every relationship that I wrote about in this book. I always feared saying no. I had an overwhelming desire to please, even when it meant not being true to myself. A little compromise for the one you love is perfectly fine from time to time. Just be careful not to lose yourself in the process because you are eaten up with the disease to please.

The disease to please makes one a perfect target to be taken advantage of, or simply taken for granted. Set boundaries. Say no. It is an empowering part of self-care.

My Need for Validation

Validation is not a bad thing. It can be affirming and positive to want your ideas, achievements, and choices validated by those around you. Recognition and acceptance of someone else's experience can be a beautiful thing. But a deep need for validation comes from a damaged ego. It is such a twisted need. We all seek validation externally, but most of us push it away when someone pays us a compliment. If you grew up feeling different or "less than," the need can run deep be hard to overcome.

So, when does validation become problematic?

My disease to please and my need for validation go hand-in-hand. It is actually my need for validation that feeds my disease-to-please affliction. I recently came to the awareness that the desire to get people to like me (my disease to please) has motivated the majority of my choices and actions, especially in my early life. But where did this strong need for validation come from? It started in my mind, and the relationSHIT with my mind that I wasn't even aware of.

How can I get to the bottom of this and heal from it? How do we heal from the root cause of the overwhelming need to feel validated and accepted?

I've had to go back all the way to my childhood to uncover where that need came from. Through the process of energy work, meditation, a lot of tears, a lot of time alone, and the support of a few amazing friends, I am still here—but I feel I might not have made it if I had continued the relationSHIT with my mind. I would not be here to write this book if I had continued to listen to, and actually believe, my mental chatter.

My journey to discovery also is requiring me to make a few difficult and painful decisions.

My need for validation and the relationSHIT with my mind has at times led me to behave in ways I am not pleased with, doing things that left me feeling more empty. My behavior has cost me some valuable relationSHIPS. Now I recognize that acting that way was a subconscious attempt to get validation and acceptance. It was just another symptom of my disease to please.

For much of my life, I have been clinically depressed. I have struggled with depression for so long, I've become very good at hiding my mood. I've always pretended everything was okay. On the outside, everything appeared okay, even though my mind was deeply troubled.

My depression stems from that feeling of not being validated and accepted. Even as far back as my early childhood, I can remember feeling depressed. Of course, at that time, I didn't know I was depressed. I just knew I felt different and out of place and sad. At a gathering, instead of having fun, I'd be sitting in a corner watching others have fun.

My father was verbally, mentally, and physically abusive, and it left me feeling unworthy, unaccepted, and not validated. This led me to seek that validation from other men. I allowed those feelings from my father to stick around for far too long. I sabotaged relationships because, embedded deeply inside, I still felt that sense of unworthiness.

I now know that I need to give myself validation and unconditional love. I've realized that, in a relationship, I have to compromise. When I'm unable to reach a compromise, I'm at the tipping point that turns the relationSHIP into relationSHIT.

One way I am moving toward self-validation (approval) is by keeping a self-appreciation journal, which has helped me cultivate a healthier relationship with my mind. Writing in the journal is a good way to begin to acknowledge the things I am most proud of about myself. The first entry in my self-appreciation journal was, "The work I do, both as a writer and nurse, makes a difference in people's lives."

So now that I've discovered where my need for validation came from, am I healed? Do I still feel the need to be validated and accepted? Do I still have the disease to please in my romantic companionships?

To answer those questions, I will say this. Self-love is a journey for me and not a destination. It is daily work. If I fail to do the work, I fall right back in to the same pattern of seeking that validation (approval) from others, which leads to a relationSHIT with my mind. I always have to work to overcome the shit and maintain a healthy relationSHIP with my mind. I have to work hard to become and remain my highest and best self.

I will continue to work at bringing more awareness to my validation-seeking thoughts and behaviors. I will continue to work on dealing with the past that led me here, in an effort to free myself and feel when someone shows me true love.

Yes, we *all* want to be accepted and validated—but it's a problem when we seek external validation as opposed to finding it within ourselves. The truth is, we don't need validation from anyone else. It is okay to be who you are. It is okay to live in your truth, no matter what that looks like. Those who truly love you will accept you in your truth.

I need to remember this every day and work on applying it to my personal life.

My Personal Affirmations:

- **I am worthy of love**
- **I am ready to receive love**
- **I validate and approve of myself**

Is the need for validation (approval) holding you back? Is the disease to please impacting your romantic companionships? Ask yourself the most important question: Are you pleasing yourself?

True Love Allows

True love is about allowing yourself to be authentic and allowing others to be who they are. It is not about controlling or trying to change anyone. True, unconditional love simply allows. Having said that, it is important not to allow others to SHIT on you. We should walk away when the SHIT starts flying. There's no room in a happy life for a relationSHIT. The disease to please and need for validation can keep you there, even though it is a relationSHIT.

There are many different philosophical views about love that we can learn from. Each of us has a unique viewpoint on what a relationship should look like, but differing does not have to mean division. Our differences can lead us to meaningful discussions. Loving and allowing also does not necessarily mean agreeing. It is perfectly fine to have different viewpoints as long as we stay respectful.

Stop trying to make your companion be what you want them to be. Stop trying to change your companion's views to line up with yours, and stop letting them mold YOU into what THEY want you to be. It takes compromise to stay together. You have to know what you are willing to tolerate, and what are the behavioral deal-breakers. You have to TRUST you can talk that out, without fear. This important lesson has led me to better relationSHIPS and kept me out of the relationSHITS. I have learned the importance of communication.

We all come from different backgrounds that influence our philosophical views and behavior. Instead of arguing over the differences, we can have meaningful, respectful discussions that help us understand one another's background and views. That's true, unconditional love.

Fully accepting someone means accepting who they are. You do not have to agree with them and you might not even understand them, but you must continue to come from a place of love. Because life is too short for hate. Life is too short for arguing, too. If today was your last day to be alive, would you spend it arguing with your companion over your different beliefs, or would you spend it just having fun with them and simply loving them? For that matter, why would you spend precious time arguing with anyone?

If you are arguing to change the other person, their beliefs are likely intolerable for you. That brings into question who has the problem. When we begin to try to change others, it's a signal that the relationship is wrong. You either tolerate your differences or you don't. The need to change the other person spells disaster is on the horizon. The shit storm is coming…

Let's take more time to listen to each other. Let's take more time to simply love and allow. Let's be respectful of others views without judging, shaming, or condemning them. This looks and feels more like a relationSHIP to me.

How beautiful a romantic companionship/relationship could be if the two involved simply loved and allowed, with zero judgment. Try it. Love and allow with zero expectations. Love and allow without projecting your own worry, stress, fear, and anxiety on your companion. Love and allow with constant, respectful communication as you both evolve.

How beautiful a romantic companionship/ relationship could be if you focused on self-improvement instead of doing a performance evaluation of your companion's life. Allow them to simply be. If their being is something that you just cannot tolerate, move on, and allow them to continue to be without you. People come and go. We must learn to embrace that change and uncertainty. Holding on because of fear is simply a relationSHIT.

What is True Love?

Love is something I find myself seeking out, falling into, and falling out of. But what exactly is true love? Is it open to interpretation by each individual, or is there only one definition? There are, of course, many different types of love, including:

- **Agape Love**: Empathetic universal love
- **Eros Love**: Romantic, passionate love
- **Philia**: Affectionate love; Intimate, authentic friendship love
- **Philautia**: Self-love
- **Storge**: Unconditional, familial love

- **Pragma Love**: Committed, compassionate love
- **Ludus Love**: Playful, flirtatious love
- **Mania**: Obsessive love

When I say "I love you," is it something I still feel or just something I say? Do I feel it every time I say it, or are they just routine words that roll off my tongue because I've been saying them to this person for a while now?

The basic, essential ideology for *True Love* to exist, from my perspective:

- **It is never our place to tell another what they can and cannot do.** This is the ultimate relationSHIT for me. We are lovers, friends, companions, or whatever the relationship is. We are not parent and child. This means it is important to have conversations and not lectures.

- **True love is unconditional.** To me, unconditional love is defined as full acceptance of another without trying to change ANYTHING about them. You can only achieve this through clear communication with your partner. If a partner is behaving in a way you can't tolerate, you have to tell them. It's YOUR PROBLEM if you don't. If you can't talk things out with your intimate partner, your relationship might be based only on the physical. Your emotions, mind, and soul cannot tolerate significant ongoing differences forever—and trying to do so can even make you ill.

Learning unconditional love is a process, and VERY FEW people can do it. If you still get upset with your partner, you are not yet fully accepting them. To love unconditionally, you must give up the need to always "BE RIGHT" or "TO WIN." Agreeing to disagree is the key.

- **Don't "should" on people**. Instead of giving them unsolicited advice, allow others to choose their own path and make their own decisions. When you make suggestions about someone else's life, you might think you're being helpful, but you're (unintentionally) saying you don't trust them to work things out on their own. Don't *should* on me, and I won't *should* on you. A little play on words, but I think you get the point.

- **True love is allowing the people in my life to be who they are**. It is not important for me to understand them or give them my permission. We are each responsible for our own happiness and wellbeing. That will look different for each of us. Just love and allow, even though they might be totally different from you.

- **Meaningful, stimulating, and intellectual conversation is vital**. When the good sex is over, what's left? The number one thing I am attracted to in another is intelligence. I find it not only sexy but an absolute necessity for me. Being able to look into one another's

> eyes and have a great conversation over dinner is priceless and over-rides everything else for me. I have often said, "The contents are much more important than the package"—even though there were plenty of times when I allowed the package to make my decisions.

I have learned that it is possible to have strong, intense feelings for someone, but not necessarily be in love with them. I have also come to realize that strong, intense feelings come from emotions. Friends can have this kind of "emotional love." Being "in love" with someone does not only mean physical love. Examining your feelings and thoughts are essential for optimal happiness and for finding the one best suited for you.

It has been hard for me to have the courage to ask myself important questions and then listen to the answers. As I have grown older, I've realized the importance of thinking about my basic, essential ideology for true love and my personal definition of true love. What is going to work for me? What it is that I want out of a relationship, and am I getting it? If not, I must listen to the answers and decide if it's worth staying, or just move on.

Romantic Companionship: What does it look like for You?

My past romantic companionships were often disturbed, and even broken, by my pre-conceived ideas about religion or other things. Sometimes, it was simply because I had no idea about what companionship should look like. What does it mean to have a romantic companion? Does it mean commitment? If so, what am I committing to?

Given the research on the high amount of infidelity and divorce, it is apparent to me that this is an issue most couples don't discuss openly. When there's an undiscussed difference of opinion in a relationship, it's often about sex.

After deep thought, I have realized that my focus has been on sex. I have tied sex to companionship. I've made sex my priority, when what I really needed was a loving companion. I could find love in good friends or even a dog, cat, bird, pig, or any pet. I have been so focused on sex that I missed out on the other beautiful aspects of a companionship. If the sex wasn't there, I threw the connection away or went looking for sex elsewhere. When the sex wasn't there, I labeled it a companionSHIT.

I grew up with the belief that one meets Mr./Ms. Right, marries them—after reciting certain unrealistic vows written by someone else—and then stays married forever. I was living my life based on someone else's idea of what my companionship should look like. That was the right and normal thing to do—right? Then it dawned on me. Why am I putting myself in this box? Why am I limiting myself to vows written by another?

The less you share thoughts and feelings openly and honestly, the more you and your companion grow apart. I could have based my companionship on open communication, and used sharing as the glue that held us together—not sex.

Society and religion are groups. Society is based on the cultural norms of the area you live in, and religion tells you how to live, based upon beliefs. You can accept the ideas of either group—or NOT. You are free to leave that religion or try to find a more accepting slice of society. Today's politics are so polarized because two groups have two totally different views of what society is. Both sides are fighting for the survival of the "soul" of America. Yet, the soul has split.

I have learned there is a fine line between dependence and independence in romantic relationships. There needs to be a healthy balance that includes dependence, but it's also important to maintain a certain level of independence. Maintaining your uniqueness is essential. There is no one else like you in the world. You have a unique purpose. You must maintain your independence so you can fulfill that purpose.

After much meditation, observation, and talking with others, I finally reached a better idea about what is best for me. My obsession with sex had led to me to believe that sex must be present for a romantic companionship to exist. But is it a sexual partner I want, or a companion? Then I reflected on my belief that it is a companion's role to love, respect, and support at all times and in ALL things. If you are vastly different, how can this happen? Choosing the right person for the right reason is key. Ideally, you will be good friends first, and then move on into the sex.

Again, the companion is there to love, respect, and support. I have found it best to just allow a companionship/relationship to be, without any interference from what society says it should be. By allowing your companion to just be, you stand in full acceptance of whatever "being" looks like for them. You're not trying to change their thoughts or behaviors in anyway. A companion's life is their journey, and I will hold their hand through that journey, without judgment.

My romantic companionship may not look like yours, and that is okay. The main goal is to live the life you love and not be put into a box or limited by another.

Chapter 9

Relationship with My Past

This is a big one for me. I have worked hard, and am still working, to leave the past behind. The past is just that....the past. There's no changing it and no going back. The past's only value is the lessons to be learned.

I have allowed past experiences to dictate my present and my future, and I've discovered that it's impossible to be present when you are in the past. We can NEVER move forward as long as we are stuck in the past.

My past experiences are tied to emotions I felt then. Every time I allowed myself to visit the past, I re-experienced the emotions. As long as I stayed in the past, my emotions also stayed in the past, and that left me feeling stuck. I have spent days crying and isolated with my thoughts completely in the past.

I have had many experiences in my life, as we all have. The death of my mother, the loss of my eighteen-year relationship, a life-threatening health diagnosis ... like everyone, I have experienced loss. We've all suffered. *My challenge has been moving beyond the suffering in my past.*

We are going to have thoughts that enter our subconscious mind related to past experiences. The question is, what do we do with those thoughts? I like the old saying, "You can't keep birds from flying over your head, but you can keep them from building a nest in your hair." You cannot keep them from shitting on your head, either. It happens. You wipe it off and move on. That is the life challenge: to let go enough to grow from all of life's experiences, good and bad.

My mom's death was traumatic for me. Every time I thought of it, I would relive the whole experience of her loss. It was painful because I was looking at it as a loss. Once I started feeling gratitude for the forty-nine years I had with her, my emotions changed. Once I started focusing on the fun times we had together, my emotions changed. The lesson for me here was, how we talk, think about, and perceive our experiences becomes the very foundation for our reality. This led to an increased awareness of my words, thoughts, and perceptions.

I am still working on moving beyond the sexual abuse I faced as a child. It has been a huge task. I began getting professional help, as my emotions were too big to handle alone. It has taken me most of my life to realize that, each time I allowed my mind to go back to that situation, I actually relived the abuse and the familiar emotions attached to those experiences. It takes work and a constant, conscious awareness to stay present and leave the past in the past. My past experience of sexual abuse has certainly impacted my relationships/shits today.

It all comes down to perception. Reflecting on the past can be good. It can show us how far we've come. It can remind us of lessons learned. Now, I can reflect on my Mother's death without becoming completely distraught. I can smile while remembering the good times. I smile when I remember her beautiful face. I can even reflect on my break-up with happy thoughts. I can reflect on the life-threatening health diagnosis I received in 1999 with gratitude, because I am not only alive, but thriving. This way of thinking has helped me to develop a healthier relationSHIP with my past.

Don't allow your past experiences to bring you down. Do what it takes to face them, deal with them, and heal from them—and then move on. Come into the present, where infinite possibilities await you. Only in the present are we able to tap into those possibilities. You will no doubt wander off occasionally, but know that you have the power and control to bring yourself back—back to the present.

Chapter 10

Relationship with the Mind

Your mind can be your worst enemy or best friend and advisor. Too often, I have allowed my mind to be my enemy. I've endured constant mental chatter, of which 99 percent is untrue. "You can't do this." "You can't do that." "You are not worthy." "You are a whore." "You are a cheater." "Your butt is too flat." All that mental chatter clogged my mind with shit. There I was, in a relationSHIT with my own mind. With a mind like that, who needs enemies?

My mind has almost talked me into ending my own life, on more than one occasion. The mental chatter has led me to actions and behaviors that I am not exactly proud of. I am working on giving all those responses back to God instead of beating myself up over them. I am giving them back to

God instead of allowing them to keep me in a relationSHIT with my mind.

It is important that the heart and mind are in alignment with each other. Listen to your heart and allow it to send the message up to your mind. I've gotten this backwards. Too often, I listen to my thoughts and allow them to dictate to my feelings. That's going in the wrong direction. Feel it in your heart first, and base your thoughts on that.

Emotions: Do They Control You?

We all have emotional challenges as we journey through this life. From the spiritual novice to the most evolved spiritual leaders, emotional challenges are unavoidable. More importantly, I have found that challenges create necessary growth and change. For that I must be grateful.

Emotions such as depression, anxiety, anger, fear, disappointment, grief, and loss affect our relationship with the mind, either for the good or the bad, healthy or unhealthy. In other words, your emotions create a relationSHIP with your mind or a relationSHIT with your mind.

I've experienced emotional challenges in my relationships with friends, co-workers, family, self, people I've dated—and most of all, with my own mind. Many of the most difficult emotional situations have been tied to the people I love the most. It hurts more with those people. I guess it's more challenging with them because of the close ties.

I made an important discovery: my emotions are directly linked to how I feel *physically*. The mind/body connection is real. *A healthy relationSHIP with mind leads to healthy relationSHIP with body.* Conversely, unhealthy relationSHIT with mind leads to a relationSHIT with the body, and this can ultimately end up in disease and illness.

My thoughts, fears, and anxieties led to my behaviors. It is important for me to be aware of those thoughts and emotions, to control my behaviors. I am finding that the more I learn to control my mind, the fewer emotional challenges I face. This helps me live in a more optimal state of being.

How do I handle my emotional challenges?

I was always taught that boys don't cry and that emotions were to be suppressed or hidden. I got used to retreating to another place, mentally, and ignoring the emotions. I still find myself doing that at times, even though I know that suppressed emotions lead to physical sickness. My outside appearance has not always reflected the state of my inside; I have suppressed the inside and smiled on the outside. If I had to bet, I'd say you've done the same.

There are no words in the universe to explain the emotional challenges I faced when I suddenly lost my mother in a car accident. Grief, loss, depression, anxiety, sadness, and anger overwhelmed me. Yet those emotions were familiar to me. I really cannot explain all the emotional challenges I have allowed to penetrate my energy field over my lifetime thus far. From simple challenges such as being frustrated with a coworker or disappointed in a family member or friend to pure anger over some situation, I've allowed negative emotions to affect my heart.

How should we handle those emotional challenges? While I am still learning, I would like to share a few tips that have helped me maintain a healthy relationSHIP with my mind:

- **Allow**: Allow those emotions to be. Recognize their existence and embrace them. It is important to ask, "Where is this emotion coming from and what is it here to tell me?"

- **Be Still**: I have learned that sometimes no reaction is the best reaction. Being still is part of allowing.

- **Breathe**: Inhale the emotion and then exhale the emotion, releasing it. The practice of breathing and focusing on that breath creates a deeper peace for me (when I am able to accomplish it.) Practice mindfully letting go as you exhale.

- **Focus on your Spiritual Being**: It is so easy to get too much into the human mind and the five senses of what we touch, smell, taste, see, and feel. We are actually spirit in a human shell, but I find myself getting that twisted every now and then. The routine practice of meditation and prayer helps put me back in touch with my spirit. It only works for me, however, when I am consistent with that practice.

This life is one big ol' classroom for me. I am learning daily. I am indeed a work in progress, and I'm acutely aware of the areas I need to continue to work on.

Dealing with emotional challenges effectively is an essential skill for a healthy relationship with the mind. I am becoming more aware that I have the power to control my internal state, completely independent of my external environment and of other peoples' opinions and behavior. It takes constant vigilance to stay aware of this truth.

Emotions are teachers if you allow them to be. Sit with them. Feel them. Are they real? I have found that, when I react and allow emotions to control me, I end up in a relationSHIT with my mind.

What if I were able to release emotions such as fear? I am able—and so are you.

Conclusion

It is my deepest hope that this book has created change and stimulated your self-healing. I hope I have prompted you to think about your relationships and how you can make them the best possible. I hope you have begun to think about how you can have relationships that lead to your highest self physically, spiritually, emotionally, mentally, and sexually.

RelationSHIPS are positive spaces where you feel loved, supported, and balanced. RelationSHITS are negative spaces where you feel unloved, not supported, and off balance. Maintain relationSHIPS and let the relationSHITS go in order to live a more peaceful, abundant, and fulfilled life. Leave the shit behind and get into a ship that is sailing forward with ease.

If you want your RelationSHIP to grow, it must be nurtured.

- Nurtured with love
- Nurtured with attention
- Nurtured with support
- Nurtured with compassion
- Nurtured with meaningful conversation
- Nurtured by being fully present. (So put down the remote, give social media a break, switch your phone to silent, and start communicating—about everything.)

Things that are not nurtured, die.

People who are not nurtured, go away.

All the relationSHIPS discussed in this book require nurturing to keep them from turning into relationSHITs.

Nurture your relationSHIPS so that you can grow in every area. Nurture your relationship with your mind, your body, and your spirit. Stay in the SHIP and out of the SHIT by simply nurturing and being aware.

I am deeply grateful to each of you for your love and support down through the years. It has been a sustaining force for me, and I send all that love right back to you. I am happy we are in a relationSHIP together.

Made in the USA
Coppell, TX
12 February 2021

50241474R00069